Crock Pot Recipes

33 Slimming Quick and Easy Crock Pot Recipes

TABLE OF CONTENTS

Copyright Notice

Disclaimer

While all attempts have been made to verify the information provided in this book, the author does not assume any responsibility for errors, omissions, or contrary interpretations of the subject matter contained within. The information provided in this book is for educational and entertainment purposes only. The reader is responsible for his or her own actions and the author does not accept any responsibilities for any liabilities or damages, real or perceived, resulting from the use of this information.

INTRODUCTION

Obesity is a major problem and people often follow different diets and slimming programs to shed extra pounds. Instead of following complicated diet programs, you can select slimming food for your weight loss. You can save money by cooking food in the slow cooker. There are numerous recipes for your assistance. The slow cooking is a method of cooking food by using low heat for a longer time. It may include Barbecues, soups, cakes, broth, etc.

Normally it takes 6 to 8 hours to prepare food in a slow cooker. You can adjust the cooker as per your needs, such as low setting, high setting and even warm setting. You need to select right ingredients because the processed oats are not good to cook in the slow cooker. You need steel-cut-oats to cook in the slow cooker for 6 to 8 hours. If you are new to slow cooking, don't worry because it is really easy and you can get numerous advantages of slow cooking.

You can prepare breakfasts, lunch, dinner and even snacks in the slow cooker. It is an excellent option for people trying to lose weight because you can get rid of additional fat without sacrificing the flavor of your food.

Slow cooking makes modest, intense cuts of meat delicate and flavorful. Most slow cooker formulas are immediately arranged and afterward left to cook for extended periods without any tension to burn food. You can set the slow cooker for 6 to 8 hours on a low setting before going to the office and your food will be ready as you return home.

CHAPTER 1 – DELICIOUS SOUPS, CURRY, AND STEWS

There are a few delicious stews and soups to enjoy for dinner. You can serve them in parties as well.

Recipe 01: Soup of Wild Rice in the Slow Cooker

- ½ cup rice, dry and wild

- 6 cups chicken stock without fat and sodium

- ½ cup onions, chopped

- 1 tablespoon butter

- ½ cup celery, chopped

- ½ pound squash, chopped

- 1 cup frozen peas, thawed

- 1 teaspoon thyme, dry

- 2 cups chicken, cooked and chopped

- Salt and pepper to taste

- ½ cup almonds, toasted

Directions:

Let the butter melt in the cooking pan on the lowest heat and add rice to cook well. Now add it to the slow cooker and add chicken stock, thyme, squash, onion, and celery. Cover the cooker for 3 to 4 hours on a low setting. Mix chicken and peas before serving and sprinkle salt and pepper. You can sprinkle almonds before serving them.

Recipe 02: Soup for Thanks Giving Meals

- 1 cup tattered turkey

- 1 cup gravy

- 1 cup crushed potatoes

- 3 cups stuffing

- 4 cups chicken broth

- 3 cups mixed vegetables

Directions:

Take a slow cooker and include turkey, potatoes, stuffing, broth, gravy and vegetables into it. Mix well to combine it and cover the cooker on a low setting for almost 4 to 6 hours. It will enhance its flavor and all the stuffing may be melted down.

Recipe 03: Turkey Broth

- Turkey bones

- 1 onion, diced

- 2 carrots, diced into large pieces

- 2 stalks of celery, chopped with leaves

- 5 whole peppercorns

- 1 bay leaf

- 3 garlic cloves, without removing peels

- 1 tablespoon vinegar, apple cider

Directions:

You need to put turkey bones in your slow cooker and add carrots, onion, bay leaves, vinegar, garlic, and celery. You can break the bones to fit them in the slow cooker. It is time to add water to one inch from the top of the cooker and cover it to cook for at least 12 or maximum 36 hours on low setting. You can keep adding water as per your needs.

Once the broth is done, let it cool and strain. Keep in the refrigerator for the whole night and skim off any unnecessary fat floated on the top. You can secure it in the refrigerator for the few days.

Recipe 04: Bean Barley Soup

- 15 ounces baked beans with tomato sauces

- 1 stalk celery, properly chopped

- 1 large onion, sliced

- 2 carrots, chopped after peeling

- 2 medium potatoes, sliced

- 6 cups beef broth (you can select vegetable broth too)

- ½ cup pearl barley, washed

- One pinch of nutmeg powder

Directions:

Take a slow cooker and mix potatoes, onion, beans, broth, celery, barley and nutmeg. Cover the slow cooker with the lid and set it on the low setting to cook for 8 to 10 hours. To cook on high setting, you can cook it for 4 to 6 hours. Season the bubbling soup with pepper and salt before serving it.

Recipe 05: Vegetable Sausage Stew

- 1 large potato, cubed

- 1 pound smoked sausage, sliced

- 1 sweet potato, cubed

- 2 carrots, chopped

- 1-1/2 cups chicken broth

- 15 ounces Italian-style stewed tomatoes, with juices

- 1 parsnip, chopped

- 1 onion, properly chopped

- 2 teaspoons sugar

- ½ teaspoon dried basil

- ¼ teaspoon black pepper powder

- ¼ cup chopped fresh basil

Directions:

Take a slow cooker and mix potatoes, parsnip, onion, sausages, basil, pepper, broth, sugar and tomatoes in it. Stir well to mix them and then cook on a low setting for 7 to 9 hours. The time for high setting will be 3 to 4 hours. Let the vegetables tender and the pricked with a fork.

Mix the parsley in the last 5 to 10 minutes of cooking and sprinkle salt and pepper to enhance the taste.

Recipe 06: Vegetable Curry/Korma

Cooking Time: 8 hours

Servings: 4 to 6

Ingredients:

- Cauliflower (break into florets): 1 large

- Chopped carrots: 2 large

- Green peas: 1/2 cup

- Chopped Green beans: 1 cup

- Chopped onion: 1/2 large

- Minced garlic: 2 cloves

- Coconut milk: 1 cup

- Curry powder: 2 tablespoon

- Sea salt: 1 tablespoon

- Garam masala: 1 teaspoon

- Red-pepper flakes: 1 tablespoon

- Almond meal: 2 tablespoons

Cooking Instructions:

Take your slow cooker and add chopped vegetables, garlic, and onion and mix all vegetables well.

Take one bowl and mix curry powder, coconut milk, garam masala, red-pepper flakes and sea salt in this bowl. Pour this mixture over vegetables and mix in almond meal. Mix them well and add any leftover ingredient in the slow cooker.

Cover your cooker and cook for eight hours on low setting and 5 hours on high setting to make the mixture thick. Serve this mixture immediately or secure in your fridge.

Recipe 07: Lamb Stew

Cooking Time: 8 hours 10 minutes

Servings: 4 to 6

Ingredients:

- Lamb (diced): 2 lb

- Spice Blend (Ras-El-Hanout): 4 tablespoons

- Diced Sweet Potatoes (peeled): 2

- Diced Apricots: 1 cup

- Diced bell pepper (red): 1

- Crushed tomatoes: 4 to 6

- Coconut Oil or Butter: 3 tablespoons

Cooking Instructions:

Take a dry and put it on the flame to roast your spice blend on hot and dry frying pan. Add lamb in the slow cooker and put all spices to coat each and every piece of lamb. Add butter and rest of the ingredients in slow cooker and mix them well. Set your slow cooker on low setting for 7 to 8 hours and cover it to cook stew. You can serve the stew with brown rice.

Recipe 08: Beef Stew

Cooking Time: 8 hours 10 minutes

Servings: 5

Ingredients:

- Pastured beef (stewing): 2 pounds

- Beef stock: 2 cups

- Balsamic vinegar: 1 tablespoon

- Chopped onion: 1 medium

- Chopped Celery: 2 stalks

- Chopped carrots: 2 large

- Cubed potatoes: 3 to 5

- Minced garlic: 3 cloves

- Paprika: 1 Tablespoon

- Bay leaves: 3

- Salt: 1/2 teaspoon

- Black pepper: 1/2 teaspoon

- Dried rosemary, oregano and basil: 1 teaspoon each

- Arrowroot powder (to make stew thick): 1/8 cup

Cooking Instructions:

Put your meat in slow cooker and add all ingredients except arrowroot powder on the top of meat. Cover slow cooker and cook for eight hours on low setting. If you want to make it thick, you have to take out maximum liquid after completing eight hours and put this liquid in one saucepan. Let it boil and put some liquid in one small bowl and mix in arrowroot powder.

Whisk it well and add in the boiling liquid cooking in the saucepan. Make sure to whisk it well to avoid any lumps. Turn off heat and there is no need to reheat after adding arrowroot powder. It can break the thick bond of your stew. If your gravy is not thick as per your requirements, you can add more arrowroot powder. Pour this thick sauce back in the slow cooker, mix gently and serve.

Recipe 09: Chicken Tortilla Soup

Cooking Time: 4 hours

Servings: 4 to 6

Ingredients:

- Olive oil: 2 Tablespoon

- Diced yellow onion: 1

- Diced bell pepper (red): 1

- Diced jalapeño: 1

- Minced garlic: 3 cloves

- Chicken (boneless and skinless): 3 to 4 breast

- Diced tomatoes: 28 ounce

- Green chiles (diced): 4 ounce

- Chicken broth: 4 cups

- Chili powder: 2 teaspoons

- Ground cumin: 1 teaspoon

- Black pepper: As per taste

- Tortilla (cut small strips): 2 to 3

Garnishing

- Cilantro (chopped)

- Guacamole

Cooking Instructions:

Preheat oil in one skillet on medium heat and sauté jalapeno, bell pepper, garlic and onion to make onions translucent. Put all these cooked vegetables in slow cooker and add remaining includes (except guacamole, tortilla and cilantro). Cook for almost 4 hours on high setting and 8 hours on low settings.

After cooking, remove chicken with the help of tongs and put on a plate or cutting board. Use 2 forks or even knife to shred chicken pieces into small bite-sized pieces. Add chicken back in your slow cooker and mix all ingredients well along with tortilla strips. Serve with guacamole and cilantro garnishing.

Recipe 10: Vegetable and Beans Soup

Cooking Time: 4 to 8 hours

Servings: 6

Ingredients:

- Green beans (chopped): 1 cup

- Carrots (Sliced): 4

- Red potato (cubed): 1 large

- Celery (chopped): 2 ribs

- Sweet onion (diced): 1/2 cup

- Corn kernels: 1 cup

- Paprika: 1 teaspoon

- Sea salt: 1/2 teaspoon

- Black pepper: 1/2 teaspoon

- Allspice: 1/8 teaspoon

- Diced tomatoes: 15 ounce

- Vegetable broth (without fat): 2 cups

- Olive oil (extra-virgin): 1 teaspoon

- Northern beans (drained): 15 ounce

Cooking Instructions:

Add all these ingredients to your slow cooker and mix them well to combine everything. Cover your cooker and cook on low setting for eight hours to tender carrots. If you want to cook on high setting, you have to cook for almost 4 hours.

In the last hour of cooking, you can remove ½ ingredients and mash them well with the help of one fork. Put these mashed ingredients in the slow cooker again and mix them well and continue cooking. It proves helpful to make your soup thick.

CHAPTER 2 – SUPERFOODS CASSEROLES

You should prepare these special casseroles, frittata and lasagna in slow cooker for lunch:

Recipe 11: Spinach Frittata

Description: You can enjoy this healthy Frittata in breakfast or with evening tea. You can serve it in party as a snack.

Cooking Time: 1 ½ to 2 hours

Servings: 6

Ingredients:

- Olive oil (extra-virgin): 1 tablespoon

- Diced onion: 1/2 cup

- Mozzarella cheese (Shredded and divided): 1 cup

- Eggs: 3

- Egg whites: 3

- 1% milk: 2 tablespoons

- Black pepper: 1/4 teaspoon

- White pepper: 1/4 teaspoon

- Baby Spinach (chopped and remove stems): 1 cup

- Diced Roma tomato: 1

- Salt as per taste

Cooking Instructions:

Take one small skillet and add oil to sauté onion for almost five minutes on medium flame.

Grease your slow cooker with cooking spray and keep it aside.

Take one large bowl and mix sautéed onion, mozzarella cheese (3/4 cup) and all remaining ingredients. Whisk them well to combine everything and put them in the slow cooker. Sprinkle leftover cheese on the top of this mixture and cover your slow cooker. Cook this blend for almost 1 to 1 ½ hours on low setting. You can insert a knife in the middle to check either it is done. If the knife is clean, your frittata is ready. Cut into slices and serve hot.

Recipe 12: Spinach Lasagna

- 4-1/2 cups spaghetti sauce, without meat and fat

- 10 ounces spinach, defrosted, chopped

- ¾ cup Parmesan cheese, grated

- 2 cups cottage cheese, without fat

- ½ teaspoon garlic powder

- ½ cup water

- 2 cups mozzarella cheese, shredded

- 1 large egg

- 1 teaspoon seasoning, Italic Flavor

- 8 ounces lasagna noodles, ready in the oven

Directions:

Take a large bowl and mix spaghetti sauce and water. Wash and drain the spinach to make it dry. Take another bowl to mix spinach, cottage cheese, parmesan, egg, garlic powder, seasoning, and mozzarella. Make a perfect blend by mixing them.

Grease your slow cooker with a cooking spray and spread ¼ of the sauce in the bottom of the slow cooker. Now add 1/3 of the noodles, spinach and cheese mixture. Make sure to cover all the noodles with the mixture. Repeat the layers twice and then spread the spinach and remaining sauce in the cooker. Cover it and cook for 4 to 5 hours on low setting. After cooking it, sprinkle remaining cheeses. Now cover the cooker and let it cook for 10 minutes to melt the cheese.

Recipe 13: Low-Carb Casserole

Cooking Time: 6 to 8 hours

Servings: 4 to 6

Ingredients:

- Coconut Oil to Grease slow cooker

- Breakfast sausage (crumbled): 1/2 pound

- Chopped bacon: 6 ounces

- Diced yellow onion: 1/2 cup

- Sweet potatoes (remove skin and shredded): 1 pound

- Bell pepper (remove seeds and diced): 1 red

- Bell pepper (remove seeds and diced): 1 Orange

- Beaten eggs: 16

- Almond milk: 1/2 cup

- Coconut milk (full-fat): 1/4 cup

- Sea salt: 1 teaspoon

- Dry mustard: 3/4 teaspoon

- Black pepper (ground): 1/4 teaspoon

- Garnishing: Green onions

Cooking Instructions:

Grease one slow cooker with coconut oil and keep it aside.

Take a skillet and cook bacon, onion and sausage in this skillet on medium heat for almost 12 minutes. Drain off extra fat and keep it aside.

Add shredded potatoes in your slow cooker and press them slightly in the downward direction. It is time to add onion mixture, bell peppers and meat over shredded potatoes (in your slow cooker).

Take a bowl and whisk milk, salt, pepper, eggs and mustard. Pour this mixture into your slow cooker and cover this cooker to set on low setting for almost 6 – 8 hours. Once it is done, cut into slices and serve with the breakfast.

Recipe 14: Crock Pot Breakfast Pie

- 8 eggs, beat

- 1lb Chicken Sausage, Torn

- 1 chopped onion

- 1 sweet potato, shredded

- 2 teaspoons basil, dry

- 1 tablespoon garlic powder

- Salt and Pepper as per taste

- Vegetables of Your Choice

Directions:

Take a crock pot and grease it with a small quantity of coconut oil. Now Shred sweet potato with shredding attachment. Add all your ingredients in the crock pot and mix well with a spoon. Set it on low setting for 6 to 8 hours to thoroughly cook sausages. You can slice it like a pie.

CHAPTER 3 – DELICIOUS RECIPES WITH CHICKEN AND BEEF

You can prepare these delicious beef and chicken recipes to serve in dinner or lunch:

Recipe 15: Roast Beef

Description: This can be a side dish or a full meal because of its delicious taste. You can cook everything in slow cooker easily.

Cooking Time: 8 to 10 hours

Servings: 4

Ingredients:

- Beef boneless (Chuck Roast): 3 lbs.

- Sweet Potatoes: 2 – 3 (cut big pieces)

- Carrots (cut big pieces): 4

- Sliced Onion: 1

- Fresh rosemary: 2 sprigs

- Bay leaves: 2

- Minced garlic: 2 cloves

- Red wine: 1 cup

- Balsamic Vinegar: 1/3 cup

- Beef stock: 1 ½ cup

- Coconut Oil: 2 tablespoons

- Black pepper (ground) and sea salt as per taste

Cooking Instructions:

Sprinkle black pepper and sea salt on the roast and keep it aside.

Melt coconut oil over medium heat in one large skillet and cook roast in this skillet for almost 2 to 3 minutes.

Put this meat in your slow cooker and top with all other ingredients. Cover your cooker and cook meat for nearly six hours on low setting.

Now add sweet potatoes and carrots in the slow cooker and cook for nearly three hours on high setting to tender vegetable and meat. Shred meat with two forks.

Discard rosemary sprigs and bay leaves and pour liquid in the slow cooker in one saucepan. Let it boil on medium heat and keep cooking until it reduces and become thick. Pour this sauce back in your slow cooker and serve with vegetables and meat.

Recipe 16: Spicy Chicken

Cooking Time: 4 to 6 hours

Servings: 4

Ingredients:

- Chicken pieces (remove skin): 2 to 3 lbs

- Ground Ginger: 1 teaspoon

- Chipotle Pepper (ground): 1 teaspoon

- Curry Powder (yellow): 2 teaspoons

- Paprika: 1 teaspoon

- Garlic Powder: 1 teaspoon

- Ground Coriander: ½ teaspoon

- Ground Cardamom: ¼ teaspoon

- Ground cloves: 1/8 teaspoon

- Cayenne Pepper (ground): ¼ teaspoon

- Ground cumin: ½ teaspoon

- Black pepper (ground) and Salt

- Cooking fat (Paleo Fat)

- Onion (sliced): 1 large

Cooking Instructions:

Take one bowl and combine chipotle, pepper, ginger, salt, cayenne, cloves, cumin, cardamom, coriander, garlic powder, paprika and curry powder in this bowl. Mix them well and rub your chicken pieces with these spices.

Grease your slow cooker and put onion slices in the bottom. Place seasoned chicken pieces over onions and cover your slow cooker. Set it to a low setting to cook for almost 4 to 6 hours to tender chicken.

You can serve with chicken with your favorite sauce.

Recipe 17: Applesauce Chicken

Cooking Time: 7 hours

Servings: 4

Ingredients:

- Chicken (cleaned and trimmed): 2lbs or 4 breasts

- Organic Applesauce (unsweetened): 2 Cups

- Onion Powder: 1/2 Teaspoon

- Garlic Powder: 1/2 Teaspoon

- Black Pepper: 1/4 Teaspoon

- Cinnamon: 1/4 Teaspoon

Cooking Instructions:

Grease your slow cooker and add all ingredients in it. Cover this cooker and cook chicken for almost 7 hours on low setting. You can serve chicken with your favorite sauce.

Recipe 18: Chicken Tacos

Cooking Time: 6 hours 10 minutes

Servings: 2

Ingredients:

- Chicken: 2 breasts

- Fresh tomatoes: 2

- Red onions: 2

- Garlic cloves: 2

- Honey: 1 tablespoon

- Basil: 1 teaspoon

- Chili powder: 1 teaspoon

- Whole cloves: 1 teaspoon

- Water: 3 tablespoons

- Lettuce leaves, red cabbage and Carrots

Cooking Instructions:

Cut tomatoes and onions into small chunks and finely chop garlic cloves.

Put chicken breasts in slow cooker and add all other ingredients in cooker including garlic, tomatoes, onion and water. Mix these ingredients with a wooden spatula and set your slow cooker to low setting for almost six hours.

Once the chicken is ready, use two forks to shred chicken and mix all vegetables and shredded chicken well. Serve with your favorite vegetables and lettuce leaves. Make sure to squeeze one lemon over chicken.

Recipe 19: Turkey Breast

- 1 onion, chopped

- 1 stalk celery, small pieces

- 1 lemon, half pieces

- 2 teaspoons olive oil

- ½ cup chicken broth

- 1 turkey breast (5 to 7 pounds)

- 1 tablespoon seasoning for steak

- 2 teaspoons seasoning for poultry

- ½ cup dry wine (white)

Directions:

Take a slow cooker and grease it. Now put the pieces of onion and celery with half lemon in the slow cooker. Take out the turkey breast and pat to dry with a paper towel. Top it with onion, lemon and celery after placing turkey breast in the crock pot. Squeeze the juice of a remaining half lemon on the turkey and add it to the slow cooker. Rub the turkey breast with olive oil and seasoning. Pour broth and wine on the turkey. Grease a large 6-Quart slow cooker. Cover the cooker and set it on the low setting for 5 to 7 hours. Check the meat with the thermometer at 165 degrees. Let the chicken breast cool for 30 minutes before shredding it with a fork.

Recipe 20: Delicious Meat Balls in Slow Cooker

- 1 pound ground beef

- 1 egg

- 1 can tomato soup

- 2 tablespoons onion flakes, dry

- ¼ teaspoon garlic powder

- Salt and pepper as per your taste

- ½ cup rice, cooked

Directions:

Take a bowl and mix ground beef, egg, salt, rice, and pepper. Prepare almost 16 balls of this mixture and place in the slow cooker in a single layer. Now add soup and cover the cooker on low setting for almost 4 to 6 hours.

Now set the meatballs in the single layer in a casserole dish and pour in the soup. Bake it in a preheated oven in a 350 degree for almost 1 hour. The meatballs will be cooked properly and the sauce becomes bubbly.

Recipe 21: Beef Vegetable and Kale in Slow Cooker

- 14 oz beef, chunks

- 2 chopped carrots

- 2 chopped onions

- ½ swede, cubes after removing the skin

- ½ celeriac, cubes after removing the skin

- Pink salt and pepper

- 6 garlic cloves

- Water

- Kale (4 handfuls)

- Potato

Directions:

In the first step, you have to prepare all your ingredients and add beef and other ingredients in the slow cooker. Add water that should be almost 2 inches deep and avoid filling the pot to the level of the brim. It is time to set your slow cooker to auto and leave it for 6 hours. Almost 15 minutes before, you can add fresh kale on the top of the cooked vegetables. Place the lid back and steam it for 5 to 10 minutes.

Recipe 22: Thai Beef in Slow Cooker

- 2 pounds beef, roast

- 13.5 ounces coconut milk

- 2 tablespoons soy sauce

- Soy sauce and hot sauce

- 10 ounces peanut sauce

- 16 ounces small carrots

- 1 red bell pepper, chopped

- ¼ cup peanuts for garnish, chopped

Directions:

Take a slow cooker and grease it with a nonstick spray. Put the beef in the bottom of the crock pot and mix the hot sauce and soy sauce together before pouring on the meat. Flip the meat several times to mix the sauces well.

Now add baby carrots and chopped bell pepper. Cover the slow cooker on low setting for almost 6 to 8 hours to make the meat tender. Once the meat is completely cooked, it is time to divide it into small pieces.

Recipe 23: Salsa Chicken

Cooking Time: 6 to 7 hours

Servings: 4

Ingredients:

- Chicken (remove fat and skin): 4 Breasts

- Green Mild Salsa: 16oz

- Water: ⅓ Cup

- Dried Parsley: 1½ Tablespoons

- Dried Cilantro: ½ Tablespoon

- Onion Powder: 1 Teaspoon

- Garlic Powder: 1 Teaspoon

- Dried Oregano: ½ Tablespoon

- Smoked Paprika: ½ Teaspoon

- Cumin: ½ Teaspoon

- Chili Powder: 1 Teaspoon

- Black Pepper: ¼ Teaspoon

Cooking Instructions:

Put chicken pieces in the bottom of your slow cooker and add rest of the ingredients on its top. Mix them well and cover this cook. Cook on low setting for almost 6 to 7 hours.

Recipe 24: Chicken Cacciatore

Cooking Time: 6 hours 15 minutes

Servings: 4 to 6

Ingredients:

- Coconut oil: 2 Tablespoons

- Minced onion: 1 large

- Tomato paste: 1/4 cup

- Dried oregano: 1 1/2 teaspoons

- Minced garlic: 2 to 3 cloves

- Red pepper (flakes): 1/4 teaspoon

- Diced tomatoes: 15 ounce

- Chicken stock: 1/2 cup

- White mushrooms (quartered): 2 lb

- Red wine: 1/2 cup

Cooking Instructions:

Take a pan and cook tomato paste, garlic, flakes of red pepper, oregano, and onion along with coconut oil in this pan. Put this mixture in your slow cooker and mix in chicken stock, tomatoes, wine, and mushrooms. Season pieces of chicken with pepper and salt and add them to your slow cooker. Mix each and everything together, cover your cooler and cook on low setting for almost 4 to 6 hours.

Recipe 25: Roast Chicken

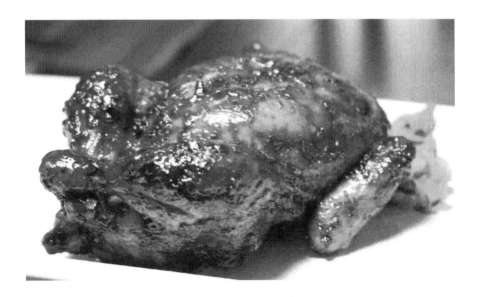

Cooking Time: 4 hours 5 minutes

Servings: 6

Ingredients:

- Whole chicken: 4-to-6 pound

- Yellow onion: 1

- Garlic: 1 head

- Lemon or orange: 1

- Paprika: 1 tablespoon

- Sea salt: 2 teaspoon

- Pepper: 2 teaspoon

- Dried thyme: 1 teaspoon

- Kitchen twine: 8 inches

- Carrots, celery or parsnips: 2

Cooking Instructions:

Quarter your lemon and onion, and cut the garlic head by cutting it from the middle.

Take a bowl and mix pepper, thyme and salt in this bowl.

Put celery, parsnips or carrots in the bottom of your slow cooker and put your chicken in the slow cooker. Sprinkle some salt mixture in the cavity of chicken and rub rest of the mixture on the top of your chicken. Sprinkle rest of the ingredients on chicken and close the lid of your slow cooker. You have to cook on high for almost four hours. You can cut the chicken into slices after cooking to serve.

Recipe 26: Chicken Chili

Cooking Time: 7 hours 5 minutes

Servings: 4 to 6

Ingredients:

- Chicken thighs (Boneless and skinless): 8 to 12

- Salsa: 16-ounce

- Italian tomatoes (diced): 16-ounce

- Chopped yellow onion: 1 medium

- Chopped red pepper: 1 large

- Chili powder: 2 tablespoons

Cooking Instructions:

Roughly chop chicken to make 1-inch pieces and put them in your slow cooker. Pour all remaining ingredients in the cooker and mix them well and put the lid on it. Set slow cooker on high for almost 4 to 6 hours and low for 6 to 8 hours. Serve with lettuce leaf or brow rice.

Recipe 27: Chicken and Mushroom Gravy

Cooking Time: 4 hours

Servings: 5

Ingredients:

- Chicken fillets (skinless): 1 1/2 pounds

- Canola oil: 2 tablespoons

- Cremini mushrooms (sliced): 16 ounces

- Yellow onion (thin slices): 1

- Minced garlic: 2 cloves

- Black pepper: 1/2 teaspoon

- Sea salt as per taste

- Chopped leaf parsley: 1/4 cup

- Chicken broth (without fat and sodium): 1 1/2 cups

- Cornstarch: 2 tablespoons

Cooking Instructions:

Add oil in slow cooker and rest of the ingredients in your slow cooker. Cover this slow cooker and set on a low setting to cook for almost 3.5 to 4.5 hours. Remove chicken and keep it aside. It is time to add cornstarch in your slow cooker and cook for almost 15 minutes. Add chicken again and mix them well. You can serve it with pasta and brown rice.

CHAPTER 4 – DESSERT RECIPES IN CROCK POT

You can prepare these delicious desserts in your crock pot. These recipes are healthy for everyone:

Recipe 28: Orange Punch

- 4 cups orange juice

- ⅔ cups sugar

- 1 lemon, piece

- 6 whole cloves

- 12-1/2 ounces lemon juice, thawed

- 4 cups water

- 2 tablespoons honey

- 2 cinnamon sticks

Directions:

Take a slow cooker and combine all ingredients in it one by one. Start with juices and then cinnamon sticks and cloves. Cover the cooker and cook on a low setting for 3 to 4 hours. Before serving, remove the cloves and cinnamon sticks and switch your slow cooker to warm setting. Equally distribute into heat-proof cups or mugs.

Recipe 29: Strawberry Punch

- 4 cups strawberry juice

- ⅔ cups sugar

- 1 lemon, piece

- 6 whole cloves

- 12-1/2 ounces lemon juice, thawed

- 4 cups water

- 2 tablespoons honey

- 2 cinnamon sticks

Directions:

Take a slow cooker and combine all ingredients in it one by one. Start with juices and then cinnamon sticks and cloves. Cover the cooker and cook on a low setting for 3 to 4 hours. Before serving, remove the cloves and cinnamon sticks and switch your slow cooker to warm setting. Equally distribute into heat-proof cups or mugs.

Recipe 30: Slow Cooker Fudge Recipe

- 2-1/2 cups Chocolate Chips

- 2 tablespoons coconut oil

- 1 teaspoon vanilla extract

- 1/2 cup coconut milk

- 1/4 cup coconut sugar or maple syrup

- Sea salt

Directions:

Take a mixing bowl and add coconut milk, salt, sugar, chocolate and oil to mix them well. Now add these ingredients in the slow cooker, cover it and let it cook for two hours on a low setting. After two hours, remove the cover of the slow cooker and add vanilla. There is no need to mix this blend at this time and let it cool to the room temperature. Use a candy thermometer to check 110 degrees temperature.

Let the mixture cool and mix it with a large spoon for 5 to 10 minutes. Lightly grease the square pan and equally pour the fudge into it. Cover it and put in the refrigerator for 4 hours or more. You can cut it into small pieces before serving.

Recipe 31: Garlic Mash

- Olive oil, 1 tablespoon

- Chicken Broth, ½ cup without salt

- 10 garlic cloves, chopped 1 tablespoon

- Plain yogurt, 1 cup

- Milk, ½ cup

- Salt as per taste

- 3 lb. russet potatoes

Directions:

Wash your potatoes and remove bad spots and peels. Make holes in the potatoes with a fork and keep all the potatoes in the microwave for 15 minutes. Remove them from the oven after they completely cooked. Cook garlic in the olive oil for 2 to 3 minutes.

Cut the potatoes into slices and put in the slow cooker with chicken broth. Keep the garlic on the top and mix everything well. Cook on a low setting for 1.5 hours and then remove the insert from the heating items. Now place the pot on the heat-safe surface. You need a hand blender to mash the potato together with the yogurt and milk. Add salt as per your taste.

Recipe 32: French Toast

- 2 egg whites

- 1 1/2 cups soy or almond milk

- 2 whole eggs

- 1 teaspoon vanilla extract

- 2 tablespoon honey

- 1/2 teaspoon cinnamon powder

- Whole grain bread, 9 slices

Ingredients for Filling:

- 3 cups apple, finely chopped

- 1 teaspoon lime juice, fresh

- 1/3 cup pecans, raw and diced

- 1/2 teaspoon cinnamon powder

- 3 tablespoon honey

Directions:

Take a bowl and add whole eggs, honey, milk, egg whites, vanilla extract and cinnamon powder to mix them well. Grease your slow cooker with the cooking spray. Add all the filling ingredients in a small bowl. Mix well to coat apple pieces and keep them aside.

Cut slices of bread into triangular shapes and start with the layer of bread in the bottom of slow cooker. Now add a 1/4th mixture of the filling mixture and add 3 layers of bread. The remaining filling will be added on the top. Pour the mixture of eggs on the bread and cover the slow cooker on high setting for

2.5 hours and low setting for 4 hours. The bread should soak the liquids. You can use bananas as a substitute of apples.

Recipe 33: Cinnamon Pancake

Description: If you like some healthy pancakes in your breakfast, you can try this healthy and delicious recipe.

Cooking Time: 1 hour 35 minutes

Servings: 4

Ingredients:

- Bisquick Mix: 2 cups

- Milk: 1 cup

- Eggs: 2

- Vanilla: 1 teaspoon

- Granulated Sugar: 3 tablespoons

- Cinnamon Powder: 1 teaspoon

- Non-stick Spray

Cooking Instructions:

Take one large bowl to mix eggs, vanilla, milk, and Bisquick to make a smooth mixture. Grease your slow cooker with non-stick spray and pour Bisquick mixture in this cooker.

Take one separate bowl and mix cinnamon and sugar together. Mix these ingredients well and sprinkle this mixture equally over batter in slow cooker.

Use end of a spoon or butter knife to swirl the sugar and cinnamon in the batter to make beautiful swirls. Cook on high setting for almost 1 to 1 ½ hours to set pancake. Serve with your favorite Syrup.

CONCLUSION

You should stay away from processed food, preservatives, toxic food and whole grains. These foods can destroy your health, and this diet can save you from all caveats of a modern lifestyle. It will help you to manage stress in your life, build muscles, reduce risks of kidney and heart diseases, boost your immune system and improve your sleeping habits by regulating body clock. It will help you to get a firm and healthy body. It is good to reduce your weight and improve your overall health.

You can try lots of delicious recipes that are easy to prepare in the slow cooker. These methods enable you to satisfy your craving without sacrificing your taste. These may not increase your weight, but you can enjoy them without any tension.

15805073R00051

Printed in Poland
by Amazon Fulfillment
Poland Sp. z o.o., Wrocław